i explore

DINOSAURS

make
believe
ideas

WHAT'S INSIDE?

Discover more about the amazing world of dinosaurs!

Dinosaurs

Stegosaurus

Ankylosaurus

T. rex

Triceratops

Deinonychus

Diplodocus

Spinosaurus

i explore facts

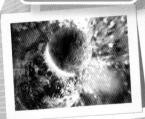

DINOSAURS

Amazing dinosaurs roamed the earth for 165 million years. All dinosaurs were reptiles, and like reptiles today, dinosaurs hatched from eggs.

Dilophosaurus

Deinonychus

(→) i learn (✕)

Dinosaurs are divided into different groups depending on when they lived. The earliest dinosaurs lived in the Triassic period. This was followed by the Jurassic period and then the Cretaceous period.

Triassic period

Jurassic period

Cretaceous period

| 250 million years ago | 200 million years ago | 145 million years ago |

Dinosaurs disappeared from the earth around 65 million years ago. Scientists think that they were destroyed by a massive meteorite or by volcanic eruptions.

Meteorite hitting the earth

T. rex

Parasaurolophus

i fact

Dinosaurs were land animals. If a creature flew, like a pterosaur, or swam, it was not a dinosaur.

Pterosaur

T. REX

Tye-RAN-uh-SAWR-us rex

teeth

jaw

Incredible Tyrannosaurus rex is one of the most famous dinosaurs. With powerful jaws filled with pointed, bone-crunching teeth, T. rex was a terrifying meat eater built to hunt!

✔ late Cretaceous period
✔ 50 ft (15.2 m) long
✔ 23 ft (7 m) tall

arm

i facts

🏠 | i facts | 🔍

ⓘ T. rex had very short arms. They were not even long enough to reach its mouth!

◯ T. rex's name means "king of the tyrant lizards."

T. rex hunting

i learn

T. rex had a massive head with jaws that stretched a huge 4 ft (0.5 m) long! It could use its jaws to grab a small dinosaur and shake it to death or bite it in two.

sharp claw

i discover

Dinosaurs can be divided into two groups, depending on how their hips were formed. Most meat-eating dinosaurs had hips that were formed like lizards' hips, while bird-hipped dinosaurs were all plant eaters.

bird-hipped

Lizard-hipped

Lizard-hipped

Bird-hipped

 i explore

✔ late Cretaceous period
✔ 26 ft (7.9 m) long
✔ 9.5 ft (2.9 m) tall

TRICERATOPS

Try-SAIR-uh-tops

Triceratops was a peaceful plant eater.
With three horns and a large, bony frill,
it had one of the largest skulls
of any land animal!

frill

horn

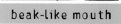

➜ i learn

Triceratops had
a parrot-like
beak that it used
to snip plants.
It had strong teeth
that could slice like
scissors through tough
leaves and branches.

beak-like mouth

12

The shape of Triceratops' frill may have shown how old it was and whether it was male or female. It may also have helped to protect Triceratops from predators like T. rex.

A Triceratops skull

⊗

Triceratops charging

⊗

leg

🏠 | i fact | 🔍

Triceratops could charge as fast as 25 mph (40 kph) to scare off an attacking dinosaur.

STEGOSAURUS

STEG-uh-SAWR-us

Stegosaurus is famous for the pointed plates covering its back. With sharp tail spikes and bony studs on its body, Stegosaurus was ready to defend itself from an attacking Allosaurus.

cheek

🏠 | i fact

ⓘ Stegosaurus ate plants using small leaf-shaped teeth in its cheeks. It could store food in its cheeks like a hamster.

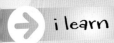

i learn

Scientists think that Stegosaurus' plates could have acted like radiators, helping it to warm up in the sun. A large male may also have used its plates to show off.

Stegosaurus in the sun

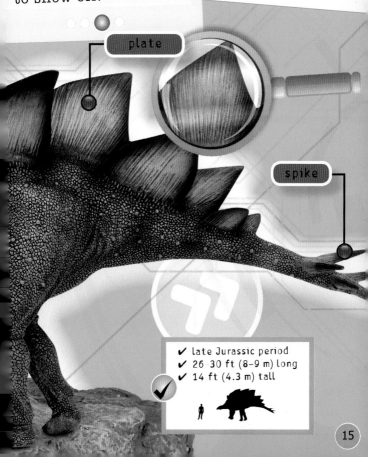

plate

spike

✔ late Jurassic period
✔ 26–30 ft (8–9 m) long
✔ 14 ft (4.3 m) tall

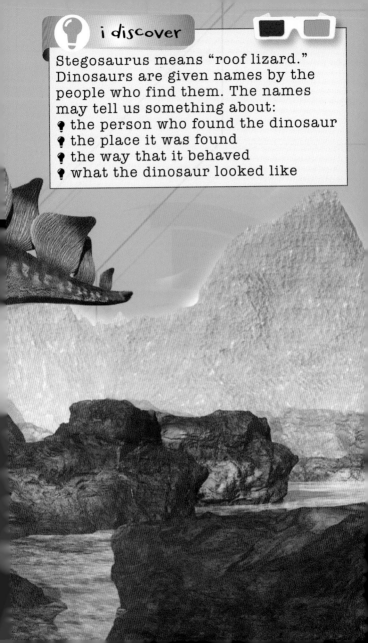

Stegosaurus means "roof lizard." Dinosaurs are given names by the people who find them. The names may tell us something about:
- the person who found the dinosaur
- the place it was found
- the way that it behaved
- what the dinosaur looked like

DEINONYCHUS

Dye-NON-ik-us

Super-speedy Deinonychus was a smart hunter with a terrifying 5 in (13 cm) cla` on each foot and about 80 sharp teeth.

teeth

i learn

Deinonychus could leap up and flick forward its large toe claws to cut into its prey. It even took its name from these fearsome features – Deinonychus means "terrible claw!"

With a large brain for the size of its body, Deinonychus was an intelligent dinosaur. It may even have been able to work in a pack to hunt down large prey.

✔ early Cretaceous period
✔ 9 ft (2.7 m) long
✔ 5 ft (1.5 m) tall

tail

🏠 | i fact | 🔍

Deinonychus and Velociraptor belonged to a group called the dromaeosaurids, who were the smartest of all the dinosaurs.

toe claw

Velociraptor

DIPLODOCUS

Dih-PLOD-uh-kus

Diplodocus was a gigantic dinosaur and one of the longest animals ever to walk on land. It had a long neck and an even longer, whip-like tail.

long neck

→ i learn ✕

Diplodocus didn't need to move around a lot to find its food. By sweeping its long neck, it could reach lots of plants while staying in one spot.

i Diplodocus' neck could grow to 26 ft (8 m) long.

Diplodocus belonged to a group of dinosaurs called sauropods. Apatosaurus and Mamenchisaurus were other massive sauropods.

Mamenchisaurus

Apatosaurus

long tail

leg

✔ late Jurassic period
✔ 89 ft (27.1 m) long
✔ 17 ft (5.4 m) tall

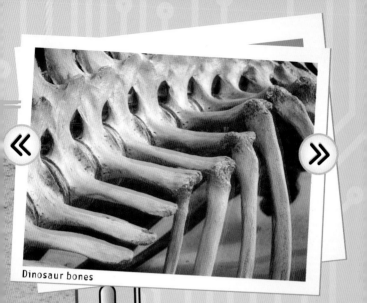
Dinosaur bones

 i discover

Although Diplodocus was a giant dinosaur, it was not as heavy as it looked. Like many dinosaurs, it had light, hollow bones, similar to those of a bird.

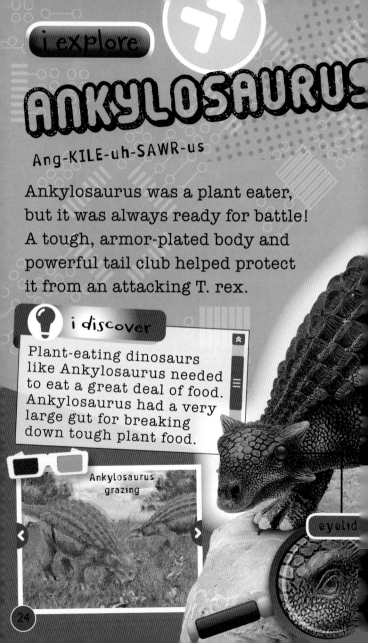

ANKYLOSAURUS

Ang-KILE-uh-SAWR-us

Ankylosaurus was a plant eater, but it was always ready for battle! A tough, armor-plated body and powerful tail club helped protect it from an attacking T. rex.

i discover

Plant-eating dinosaurs like Ankylosaurus needed to eat a great deal of food. Ankylosaurus had a very large gut for breaking down tough plant food.

Ankylosaurus grazing

eyelid

24

Ankylosaurus could swing its dangerous tail club from side to side. Made from bone, the club was strong enough to break the bones of another dinosaur.

○○●○○

tail club

armored plate

🏠 | i fact 🔍

Ankylosaurus was so well protected, it even had bony plates on its eyelids! It could flick its bony lids up and down to cover its eyes.

✔ late Cretaceous period
✔ 35 ft (10.6 m) long
✔ 11 ft (3.4 m) tall

SPINOSAURUS

SPY-nuh-SAWR-us

Gigantic Spinosaurus may have been the largest of all the meat-eating dinosaurs that walked the earth. With sharp teeth and claws, Spinosaurus hunted fish in lakes and rivers.

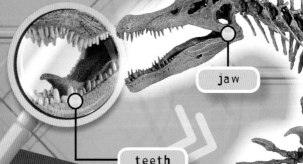

jaw

teeth

- ✔ Cretaceous period
- ✔ 40 ft (12.2 m) long
- ✔ 16.5 ft (5 m) tall

Spinosaurus had a mouth full of long, cone-shaped teeth, perfect for grabbing wriggly fish and stopping them from escaping its crocodile-like jaws!

Spinosaurus

spine

law

🔍 i facts

ℹ️ Spinosaurus' name means "spiny lizard."

⭕ The spines on Spinosaurus' back could be as tall as 6 ft (2 m), which is taller than many adults!

sail

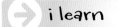
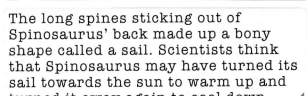

The long spines sticking out of Spinosaurus' back made up a bony shape called a sail. Scientists think that Spinosaurus may have turned its sail towards the sun to warm up and turned it away again to cool down.

i explore FACTS

The most complete T. rex skeleton stands in a museum in Chicago, Illinois, and it's called Sue. Despite this, experts don't really know whether it was male or female!

The largest dinosaur eggs discovered were thought to have weighed up to 15 lb (7 kg) – that's about the same weight as 140 chicken eggs!

When Triceratops' horns were first discovered, they were thought to have belonged to a very large bison!

Brachiosaurus was a gigantic sauropod. Its long neck was twice the length of a giraffe's neck!

Only Ankylosaurus' soft armpits were free from armor. But if it were flipped onto its back in an attack, it would have been easily wounded.

Parasaurolophus used the large, hollow crest on its head to make hooting sounds that warned its herd of danger.